International Baccalaureate
Biology
Option
Evoluti

Introduction

Welcome to the International Baccalaureate Evolution Revision Guide.

The layout is similar to the main guide with the key points highlighted and summarised. Once again there are numerous revision questions within the text.

Statements are in pale blue boxes.

Statement

There are very few definitions in the Options and so these have been incorporated in the text in pink boxes.

Definition

In the top right hand corner of the page are green boxes that give the heading for that sub division of the Option.

Origin of Life

A commonly used and accepted abbreviation used in this guide is **mya** meaning millions of years ago.

I am extremely grateful to The Corrian Homan Design Studio for the gradualism diagram on page 12.

In particular I am greatly indebted to Tony Stuart and Peter Bowen-Walker for their advice and assistance, and also to Dick Vane-Wright.

Once again I would greatly value any feedback on this revision guide so that later editions can continue to help students throughout the world. Please feel free to email me at Oxford Study Courses – osc@osc-ib.com.

Ashby Merson-Davies.

Option D

Evolution

Core Material

❖ Origin of Life on Earth

Spontaneous origin of life

Investigations such as those by Pasteur in the 19th century showed that all life comes from life, ie it cannot appear spontaneously. However the early Earth was sterile and so organic molecules must have formed and then become organised into cell-like structures.

Processes

1. Non-living synthesis of simple organic molecules.

   Simple organic molecules would include sugars, amino acids, nucleic acid bases.

2. Assembly of these molecules into polymers.

   Simple polymers would include polysaccharides and polypeptides.

3. Origin of self-replicating molecules that make inheritance possible.

4. Packaging these molecules into membranes with an internal chemistry different from their surroundings.

Miller and Urey (1953)

Key facts

- Simulated what was thought to be the Earth's pre-biotic atmosphere and conditions;
- Atmosphere was a mixture of ammonia, methane and hydrogen;
- It would have been hot and with many electrical storms;
- After several days liquid became brown;
- Analysis showed presence of several organic compounds including sugars, amino acids and nucleic acid bases.

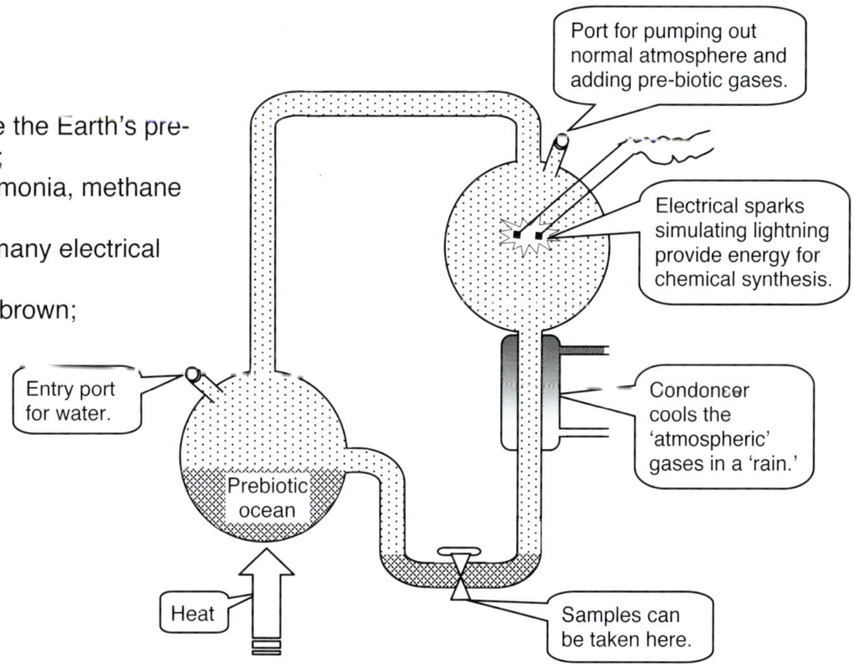

Possible locations of organic synthesis

1. The Role of Clays

Points for discussion

- The large complex molecules of life require stable conditions in which to form;
- Clay minerals such as silicic acid can form sheets with narrow spaces between that can hold other molecules close together allowing reactions to occur;
- Clays can act as catalysts for other polymerisation reactions such as formation of polypeptides from amino acids.

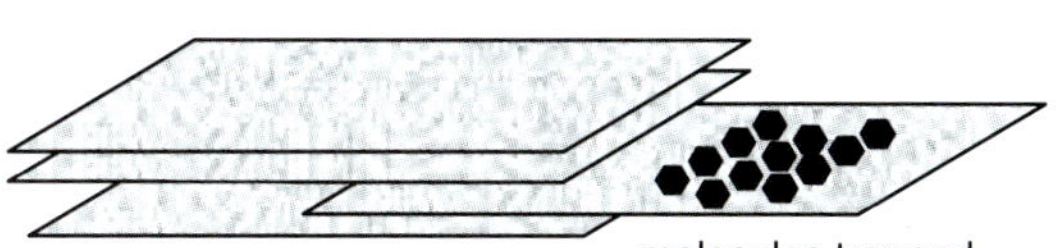

2. Hydrothermal vents

Points for discussion

- These are extremely deep in the oceans and are where the volcanic eruptions are contained due to the immense pressure;
- The water close to the vent is warmed and rich in minerals coming from the vent;
- These unusual conditions could have allowed organic molecules to form.

A hydrothermal vent on the floor of the Pacific Ocean injects superheated steam and hydrogen sulphide (H_2S) into the environment. Archaea (bacteria) that use the H_2S for energy are found near such thermal vents growing at temperatures as high as 120°C.

3. Volcanoes

Points for discussion

- Hot springs in volcanic regions on the Earth's surface are also very rich in minerals and are where organic compounds could form;
- High concentrations of these compound could build up helping the formation of polymers.

Opalescent Pool in Yellowstone National Park, Wyoming USA. In these types of hot springs, the orange, yellow and brown colors are due to pigmented photosynthetic bacteria which make up the microbial mats. The mats are literally teeming with bacteria. Other non-photosynthetic bacteria, as well as various archaea and algae are also residents of the hot spring community.

4. Extra-terrestrial

Points for discussion

- Scientific investigations since Miller and Urey have shown that organic compounds can form in space;
- The cold temperature of space reduces molecular movement which encourages the formation of polymers;
- These molecules could have been brought to Earth by comets, meteors and cosmic dust which rained down on the early Earth.

Comets may have delivered organic compounds to Earth.

The Possible Role of RNA

Points for discussion

- RNA, like DNA, is a sequence of nucleotides that can carry a genetic code;
- It is structurally simpler than DNA;
- It can replicate itself;
- It has some enzyme functions for catalysing other reactions, eg formation of the peptide bond in polypeptide formation in the ribosome;
- In eukaryotic organisms today RNA plays many significant roles in the genetic control and regulation of the cell.

Protobionts

Living cells may have been preceded by protobionts with an internal chemical environment different from their surroundings.

Protobionts include coacervates and microspheres.
Under certain situations these can replicate, absorb substances to form higher concentrations inside, carry out chemical reactions, and releases substances. In this way they show some characteristics of life but cannot be described as living.

- Microspheres
  - Simple spheres of polypeptide.
- Coacervates
  - Aggregates of amino acids, proteins, and polysaccharides surrounded by a tight skin of water molecules. Lipids may form around them to form a membrane-like structure.

Prokaryotes and Oxygen

Key facts

- The early atmosphere was anaerobic;
- Early forms of prokaryotic photosynthesis, combining carbon dioxide and hydrogen to form carbohydrate, used hydrogen sulphide, H_2S, as the hydrogen source;
- Sulphur was the waste product and can be seen as yellow deposits around volcanic vents;
- This limited the prokaryotes to volcanic regions where hydrogen sulphide fumes escaped from the rocks;
- Modification of the photosynthetic pathway allowed the use of hydrogen oxide, H_2O, (water) as the hydrogen source;
- The waste product, oxygen, gradually accumulated in the atmosphere allowing the evolution of the much more efficient aerobic respiration pathway;
- Living forms of photosynthetic prokaryotes are called Blue-green bacteria or Cyanophyta.

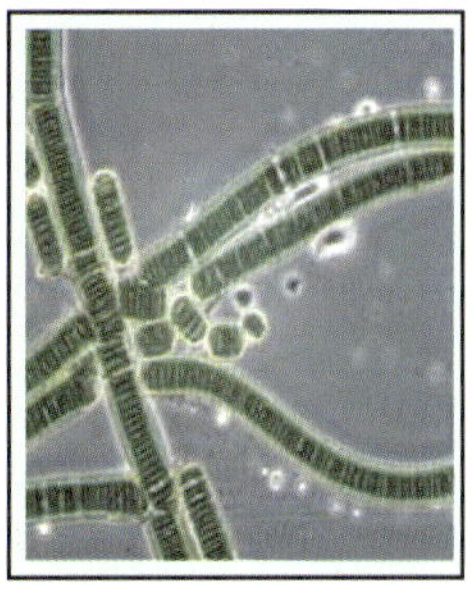

Blue-green bacteria or Cyanophyta.

The Endosymbiotic Theory

Points for discussion

- This theory is that eukaryotic cells arose from combinations of different types of prokaryotic cell.
- Usually, if one type of bacterial cell gets inside another, one of two things happens:
  - the host cell digests the invader;
  - the invader multiplies and kills the host cell.
- Thus, there is a battle between host and invader.
- The endosymbiotic theory imagines a drawn result – neither host nor invader wins and they settle down to work together;
- Suppose three types of imaginary prokaryotic cell which we will call 'Eater', 'Eliminator', and 'Sunshine' –

'Eater'
The first is a good eater – it is very effective at swallowing other types of cell and digesting them. But it is restricted to places where there is no oxygen since it does not have the ability to eliminate this reactive substance.

'Eliminator'
The second has acquired the trick of eliminating oxygen very rapidly. This means that it can occupy places where 'Eaters' are scarce.

'Sunshine'
The third has opted out of eating altogether – it has acquired the trick of making its own organic molecules using the sun's light energy. As a by-product it excretes oxygen.

These still exist as blue-green bacteria.

Remember that the early Earth was almost entirely anaerobic so 'eaters' would have evolved first.

Eater swallows *Eliminator*. Good for *Eater* – *Eliminator* gets rid of oxygen effectively and so it can go places where other *Eaters* can't and so eat even more. Good for *Eliminator* – no other *Eater* can eat it and it has a supply of food provided by *Eater*. These types could provide the basis of the **animal kingdom**.

Eater plus *Eliminator* swallows *Sunshine*. *Eater* can relax and have its food made for it from now on. To stop other *Eaters* tackling it, it might use some of its food to make a tough wall of cellulose. These types could provide the basis of the **plant kingdom**.

'Eliminator' became the mitochondrion;
'Sunshine' became the chloroplast.

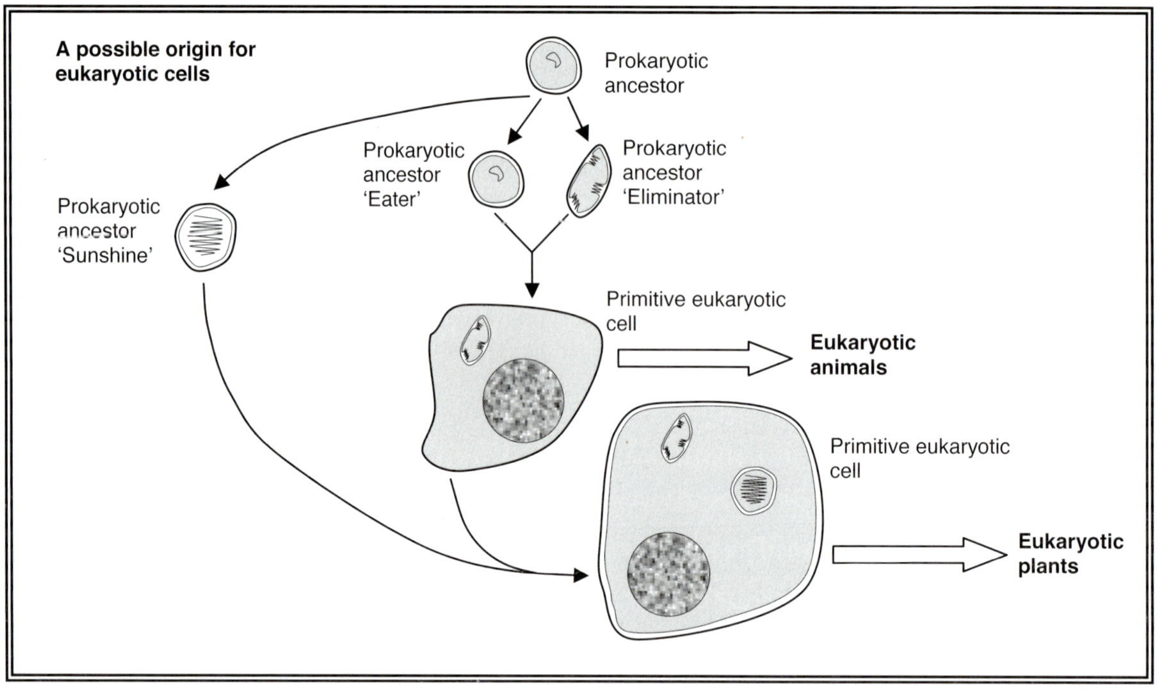

Evidence :-

- Chloroplasts and mitochondria both have envelopes (double membranes). The inner membrane would be that of the prokaryote that had been eaten, and the outer membrane would be formed around it from the plasma membrane of the eating prokaryote. (Revise endocytosis – phagocytosis);
- Chloroplasts and mitochondria have a loop of naked DNA as in prokaryotes;
- Chloroplasts and mitochondria can divide independently from the cell;
- The ribosomes in chloroplasts and mitochondria are the same size as those in prokaryotes (70S), and smaller than those in eukaryote cytoplasm (80S);
- Thylakoids are similar to the structures found in blue-green bacteria;
- Chlorophyll *a* is the main photosynthetic pigment for both prokaryotes and eukaryotes;
- Mitochondrial cristae are similar to mesosomes, folded structures formed from the plasma membrane of prokaryotes and where respiration takes place.

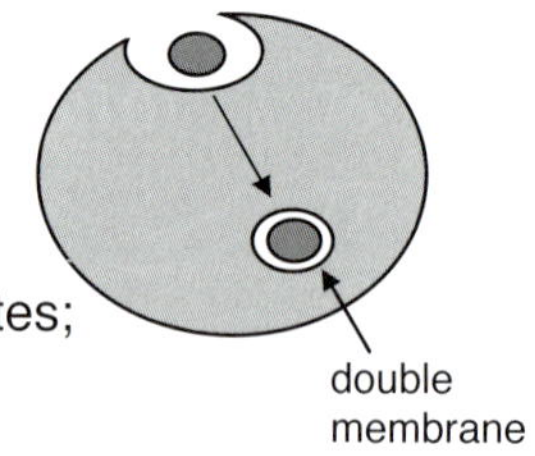

List the four processes needed for the spontaneous origin of life on Earth.

Outline the Urey-Miller experiment and results.

List three locations where conditions would have allowed the synthesis of organic molecules.

Outline two properties of RNA that would have allowed it to play a role in the origin of life.

Outline the contribution of prokaryotes to the formation of an oxygen-rich atmosphere.

Outline the endosymbiotic theory.

❖ Species and Speciation

Gene pool
All the different genes in an interbreeding population.

Allele frequency
The frequency of a particular allele as a proportion of all the alleles in a population.

Evolution involves a change in allele frequency in a population's gene pool over a number of generations.

Allele frequency can range from 0.0 to 1.0. It might seem odd to have a frequency of zero, but remember it applies to a population – the allele might be present in a different population of that species. Differences in allele frequencies can lead to speciation.

Defining the Term 'Species'

Points for discussion

- As more of the planet was explored more and more species of plants and animals were sent back to major museums for classification;
- At first all that could be done was to describe the appearance of the organisms;
  - This was the **monotypic species**:
  - This led to errors such as one 'species' of butterfly having only males and another 'species' having only females. They were of course the same species but very different in appearance;
- As more information was gathered about differences between males and females, young and adult, winter and summer forms, regional differences, the descriptions enlarged;
  - This was the **polytypic species**:
- As the descriptions came to include behaviour and genetics the definition was changed to the current view;
  - This was the **biological species**:
- There are several difficulties with this –
  - Populations separated by time cannot interbreed – a butterfly in 2009 cannot breed with a butterfly in 2015.
  - Populations separated by space may not be able to interbreed – a snail in Poland cannot breed with a snail in Hungary.
  - Fossils clearly cannot breed and their numbers may be too few to determine whether differences are due to speciation or to normal variation within the species.
  - Some fossils, such as those in the Burgess Shales, bear no resemblance to anything living or to any other fossil, eg *Hallucigenia sparsa*.
  - The biological definition cannot be applied to species that only reproduce asexually.
  - A species may show a gradual change in phenotype, a cline, over its range. eg the *Larus* gull cline described on the next page.

A species.
Groups of actually or potentially interbreeding natural populations which are reproductively isolated from other such groups.

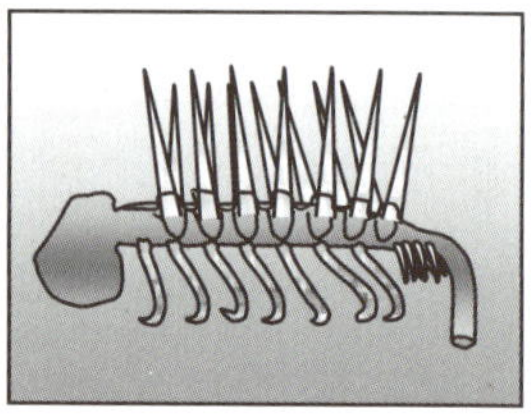

Hallucigenia sparsa from the Burgess Shales

Speciation

Key facts

- This is the evolution of one species into another;
- There are two forms –
  - Sympatric means in the same geographical area;
  - Allopatric means in different geographical areas;
- A break-away population can be formed during migration;
  - eg. a storm blowing a group of birds off route (possibly Galapagos finches) or a group being left behind when the main population moves.
- The break-away population, being small, is likely to have a different balance of alleles from the main population;
- This could make it more susceptible to different selection pressures;
- For speciation to occur the populations must be separated by some barrier to gene flow;

Remember – 'sym' means together, as in 'symbiosis – living together.

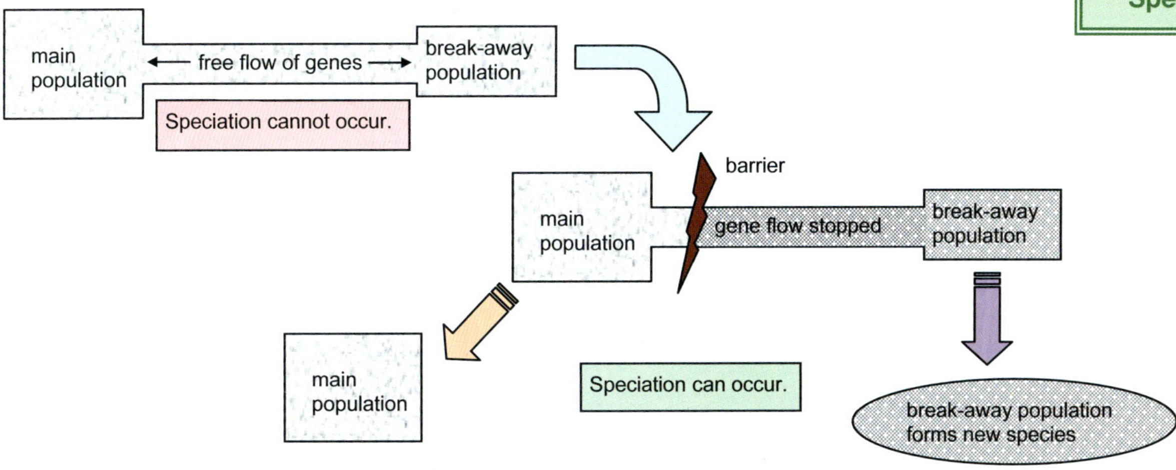

Barriers Between Gene Pools

Sanguinus fuscicollis fuscicollis photgraphed by Roy Fontaine at Monkey Jungle, Miami, Florida. Reproduced by kind permission of the photographer Roy Fontaine.

- **<u>Geographical</u>**, eg. water, mountain range:
  - Example of **sympatric speciation** – the saddle-backed tamarin on the banks of the Rio Jurua in western Brazil;
  - Tamarins on the west bank have dark coats and belong to the subspecies *Sanguinus fuscicollis fuscicollis;*
  - Tamarins on the east bank have pale coats and belong to the subspecies *Sanguinus fuscicollis melanoleucus;*
  - In places where the river breaks through a wide meander a group of west bankers may find itself on the east bank and vice versa;
  - In such cases hybrids form between the two subspecies;
  - Over a longer period of time more genetic differences may occur and the subspecies may become separate species.

- **<u>Behavioural</u>** eg different calls and courtship behaviour:
  - Example of **sympatric speciation** – *Larus* gull ring cline.
  - These birds form a ring of 10 subspecies around the North Pole. Each subspecies can interbreed with the adjacent ones except in the British Isles, Netherlands and Germany where the two 'ends' of the ring meet.

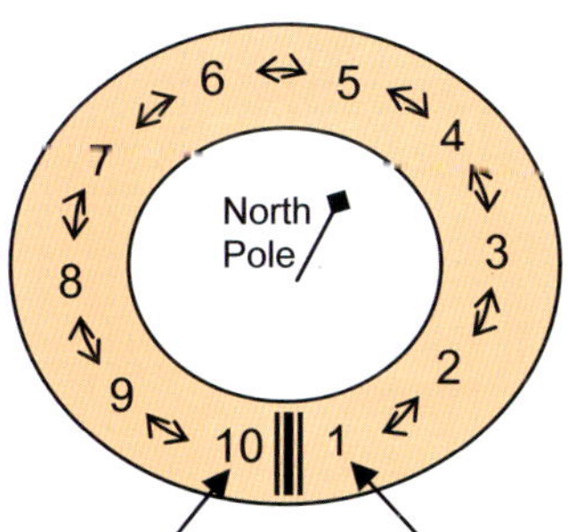

lesser black-backed gull *Larus fuscus*

herring gull *Larus argentatus*

⇔ interbreeding can occur

|| interbreeding can, but rarely does, occur because species 1 and 10 differ in appearance, call, and migratory pattern.

Herring gull
Grey back and pink legs

Lesser black-backed gull. Black back. Winter adults have pink legs; summer adults have yellow legs.

Photographs by the author.

- The original species probably spread in one direction (in the diagram this would be anticlockwise) and selection produced minor variations along the way. When the end of the ring closed back at the starting point there was so much variation between the starting form and the final form that interbreeding was inhibited.

- **Temporal** ie found in the same habitat but at different times.
  - Two British moths, The Common Marbled Carpet (*Dysstroma truncata*) and The Dark Marbled Carpet (*Dysstroma citrata*) would interbreed if raised together artificially;
  - In the wild they do not interbreed because *D. citrata* is on the wing in July / August but *D. truncata* is on the wing in May / June and then again in September / October.

	May	June	July	August	September	October
D. truncata						
D. citrata						

Polyploidy and Speciation

Key points

- 'Ploid' is the name given to a set of chromosomes. Thus diploid is two sets, triploid three sets, etc.
- Polyploid is a general name for more than two sets. (Diploid is the norm).
- During sexual reproduction chromosomes must pair up during meiosis. (See core guide p56/7).
- Thus there must be an even number of chromosomes.
- During embryonic mitosis a mutation may occur where all the chromosomes fail to separate at anaphase resulting in a tetraploid cell, leading to a tetraploid organism.
- Meiosis in a tetraploid cell results in a diploid gamete.

Parent	diploid	x	diploid	x	tetraploid	x	tetraploid
Gamete	haploid		haploid		diploid		diploid
Offspring		diploid		triploid		tetraploid	
Fertility		fertile		sterile		fertile	

- Since the triploid hybrid is sterile it acts as a barrier between the diploid and tetraploid forms and over time other differences could accumulate leading to speciation.
- An example is the cord grass *Spartina*. *S. alterniflora* has a diploid number of 62. *S. maritima* has a diploid number of 60. The hybrid *S. x townsendii* has a diploid number of 61 and is sterile. (A mutation later occurred where the chromosome number doubled to 122 and this form, *S.anglica*, is fertile).

Adaptive Radiation

Key points

- As speciation occurs a particular structure may change to become adapted to a particular requirement and carry out very different roles;
- When anatomical parts share the same underlying pattern of number/arrangement they are said to be *homologous*.

Example

- **The pentadactyl limb;**
  - So called because it typically has five digits;
  - Found in all four classes of terrestrial vertebrates – amphibians, reptiles, birds and mammals.

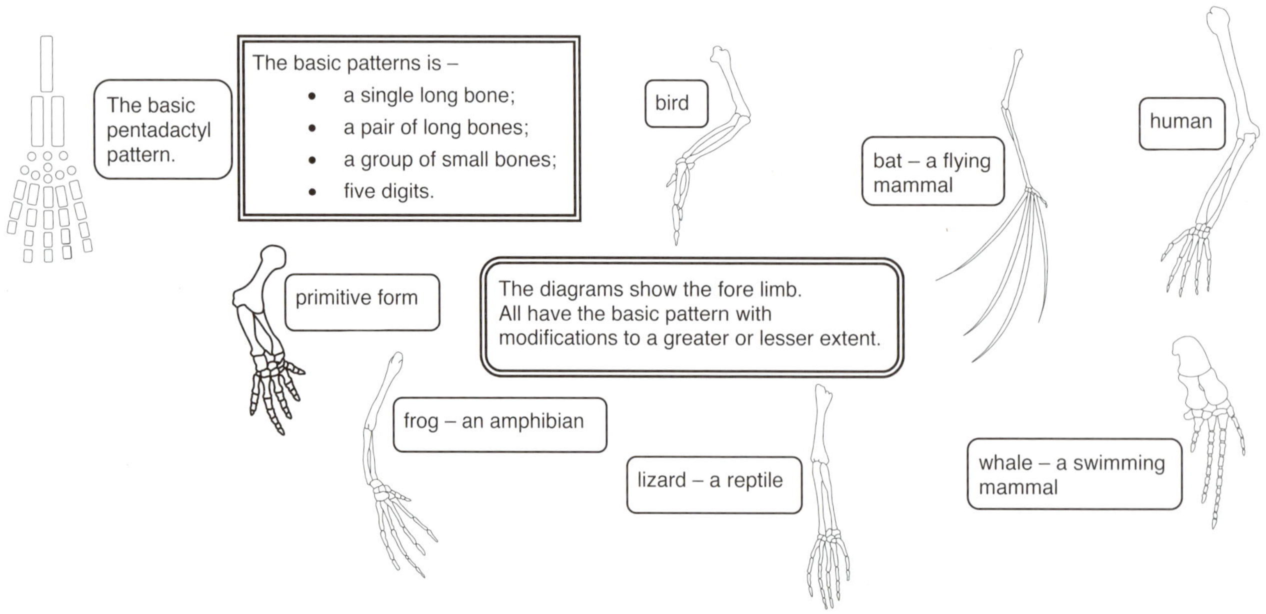

Divergent and Convergent Evolution

Key facts

Divergent evolution is when a common ancestral structure diverges into a range of different structures which may or may not have the same function; Example - the pentadactyl limb on the previous page.

Convergent evolution is when different ancestral structures give rise to features that resemble each other because they carry out the same function. Example 1 - Wings of bats and insects.

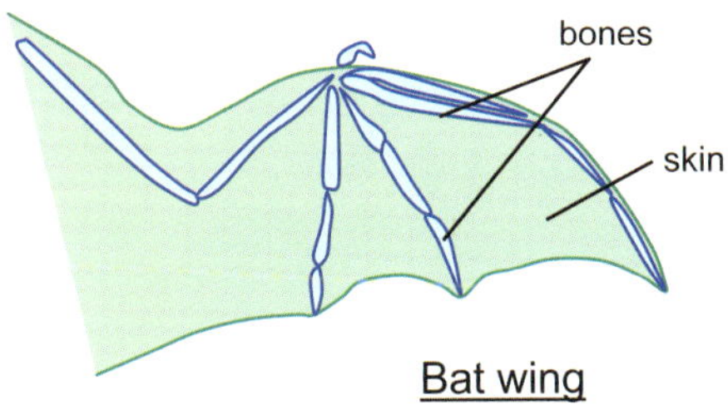

Bat wing

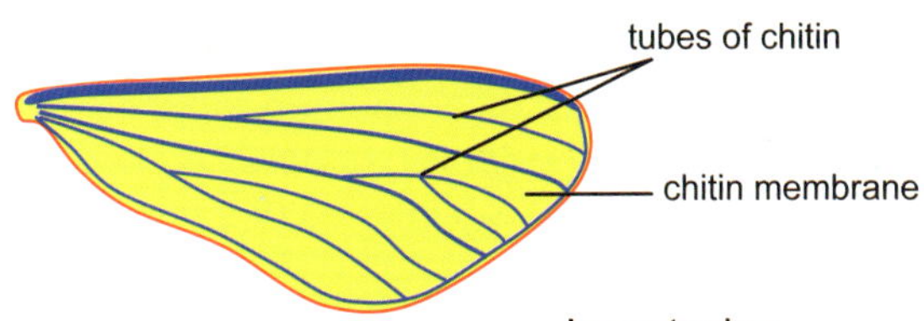

Insect wing

Example 2

- Mimicry is an interesting example of convergent evolution.
- If an insect tastes nasty then birds will quickly learn this and avoid them.
- If two nasty tasting butterflies mimic each other then a bird will only need to taste one of them to learn this and so both species are protected.
- If nice tasting species mimic the nasty tasting ones then they are also protected.
- All four species shown are found in the lower Amazon basin.

Methona confusa

Lycorea ilione

These are both distasteful members of the butterfly family *Nymphalidae*, Order *Danainae*.

Patia orise

This is a tasty member of the butterfly family *Pieridae*.

Gazera linus

This is a tasty member of the day flying moth family *Castniidae*.

Reproduced by kind permission of the Natural History Museum, London

The pace of evolution – Gradualism and Punctuated Equilibrium

Gradualism
A slow change from one form to another.

Punctuated equilibrium
Long periods with little change with intermittent short periods of rapid change.

Points for discussion

- Gradualism is a Darwinian approach;
- The fossil record indicates this to be true in some cases, eg the horse leg where the fossils show all the stages from the earliest horse to the modern horse;
- In other cases the fossil record shows no intermediates;
- Eldredge and Gould proposed that most evolutionary changes take place at the time of speciation;
- Small populations that become isolated do not contain the full gene pool and have different allele frequencies;
- Environmental differences encourage rapid speciation in these small populations and once established new genotypes resist change;
- The population enters a long period of stasis until punctuated by another change;
- An example of this would be the variety of Darwin's finches on the volcanic Galapagos Islands;
- Sometimes these changes can affect local populations such as a rise in sea level creating an island, or a major volcanic eruption that affects the global climate, eg after Krakatoa erupted in 1883 average global temperatures fell by 1.2^{0}C.

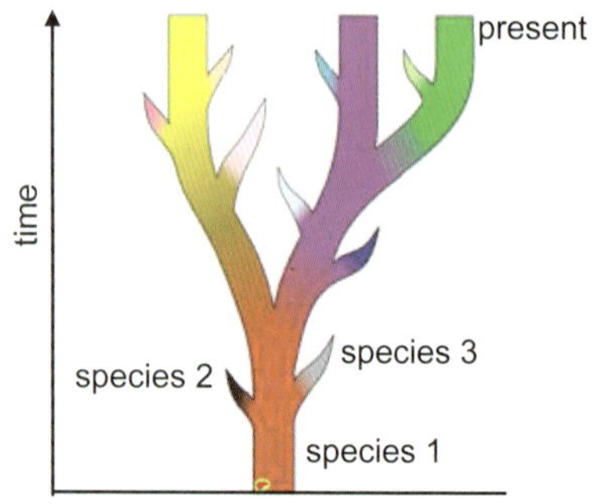

Gradualism

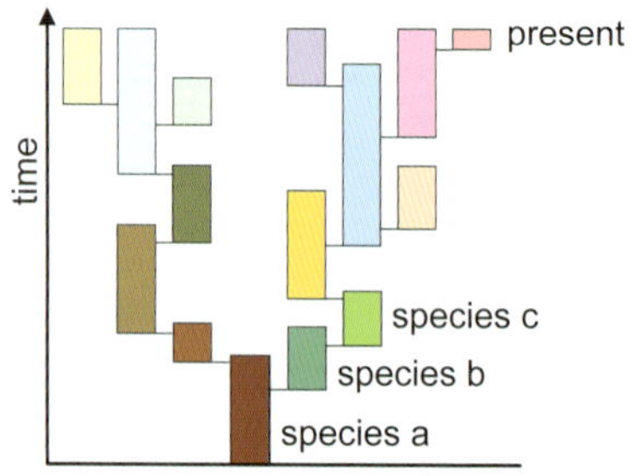

Punctuated equilibrium

Polymorphism

Key facts

- Polymorphism is the existence of two or more forms within a population such that the smallest of them could not be maintained by mutation alone.

<u>Balanced polymorphism</u>

- Example – sickle-cell anemia;
- This is a codominant genetic disorder and thus there are three genotypes – normal ($Hb^A\ Hb^A$), sickle-cell trait ($Hb^A\ Hb^S$), sickle-cell anemia ($Hb^S\ Hb^S$);
- Sickle-cell anemia is a serious disease which is often fatal because all of the red blood cells are affected;
- Thus there is selection pressure to eliminate the allele;
- Sickle-cell trait only causes mild anemia;
- Sickle-cell trait gives great resistance to the most virulent form of malaria;
- In regions where malaria is endemic (naturally occurring) there is selection pressure against $Hb^A\ Hb^A$ (you die from malaria) and $Hb^S\ Hb^S$ (you die from anemia) but selection pressure for $Hb^A\ Hb^S$ (you may have mild anemia but don't die from malaria);
- This leads to a balance in the proportions of the three genotypes in the population.

Balanced
This means that the all the forms remain at stable levels in the population.

<u>Transient polymorphism</u>

- Example – The Peppered moth *Biston betularia*. This moth is common in England;
- The normal form has white wings covered in black specks;
- Dark forms in which the black specks had merged to varying degrees first appeared during the industrial revolution during the mid 19th century;
- The moth rests during the day on lichen covered tree trunks and the normal form would be well camouflaged;
- As the trees near industrial areas became dirty with soot the dark forms would be camouflaged but the normal speckled form would be easily seen and eaten by birds;
- In clean country areas the dark form would be seen and eaten;
- This led to a transient polymorphism in industrialised areas as the population of the dark form increased and that of the speckled form decreased.

Transient
This means that the additional forms only exist in the population temporally.

- Then came a period of balanced polymorphism;
- In 1956 the Clean Air Act was passed and gradually the soot was washed off the trees;
- Selection pressure started to work against the dark forms and over the next 30 years transient polymorphism moved in the opposite direction.

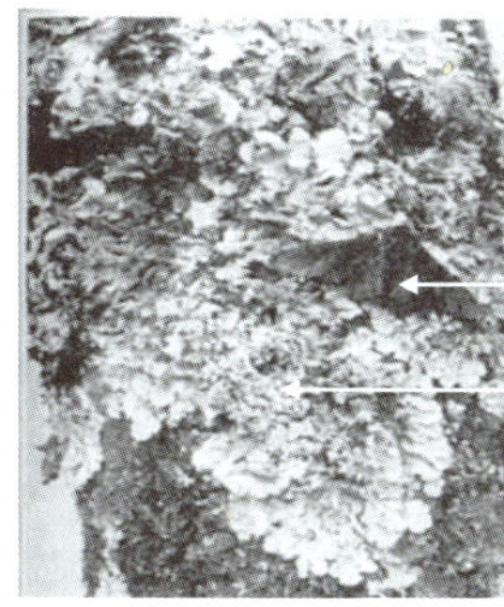

On a lichen covered tree trunk the normal form is well camouflaged.

On a soot covered tree trunk the dark form is well camouflaged.

Interestingly sickle-cell anemia is showing transient polymorphism amongst the black population in the USA. Many of their ancestors who were $Hb^A\ Hb^S$ were taken as slaves to the USA. Malaria is not endemic in the USA and so there was no selection pressure for the Hb^S allele. Thus there has been a gradual decrease in the frequency of the Hb^S allele and hence a change in the proportions of the three genotypes amongst the black population.

Define allele frequency.

Define gene pool.

List at least six points for discussing the definition of a species.

Describe three examples of barriers between gene pools.

What is speciation?

What is polyploidy? How can polyploidy lead to speciation?

Compare allopatric speciation with sympatric speciation.

What is adaptive radiation? Give an example.

Compare convergent and divergent evolution. Give an example of each.

List 6 points to be used in a discussion on the pace of evolution.

What is polymorphism?

Describe one example of balanced polymorphism.

Describe one example of transient polymorphism.

❖ Human Evolution

Dating Rocks Using Radioactive Decay

Key points

- Elements can exist in different forms called isotopes;
- Some of these isotopes are radioactive and decay (change) into other isotopes (by giving off radioactive particles or waves);
- The half-life of an isotope is a constant for that particular isotope;
- This value can be used to date a fossil or the rock in which it was found;
- Radioactivity is easy to detect and to measure.

Half-life
The time period for an isotope to decay to half its original mass.

Carbon dating

Key facts

- The normal form of carbon is ^{12}C;
- The radioactive form is ^{14}C;
- The half-life of ^{14}C is about 5700 years;
- It is useful for fossils that have not turned to stone and are between 10^3 and 10^5 years;
- In an organism's lifetime it makes, or eats, organic material to incorporate into its body;
- Thus, the carbon atoms that form the basis of this organic material are in a ratio that is identical with the naturally-occurring background ratio of the carbon atoms in carbon dioxide in the air;
- When the organism dies, it stops incorporating organic material;
- Any radioactive carbon it contains will then decay;
- We can then use the % decay curve as shown on the right.

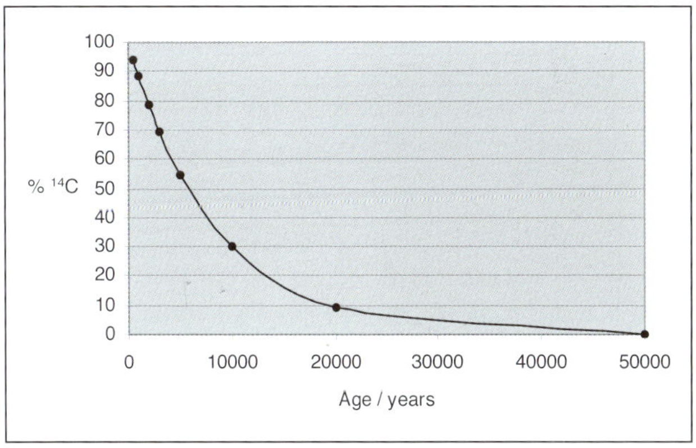

Potassium-Argon dating

Key facts

- The radioisotope potassium-40 (^{40}K) is rare and decays to the inert gas argon-40 (^{40}Ar);
- The half-life of ^{40}K is about 1.3 billion years;
- It is used to date older fossils, a million years old (or older), or the rocks in which they are embedded.
- The argon gas is trapped in the rock which contained the potassium;
- The argon gas is released from a sample and the ratio of parent atom ^{40}K to the daughter atom ^{40}Ar is measured as shown in the graph below.

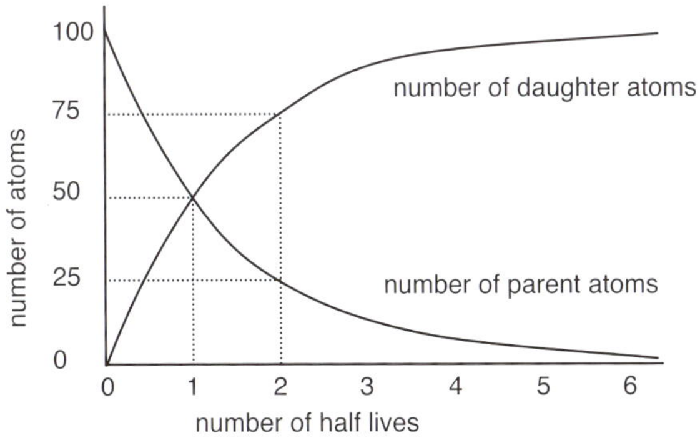

The proportion of parent to daughter atoms tells us the number of half lives that have passed since the organism died. For example if there are equal numbers of parent and daughter atoms then 1 half life has passed; if there are three times more daughter atoms than parent atoms then two half lives have passed.

Humans as Primates

Key Features

➢ Primates share the following physical features which are adaptations to a tree-dwelling lifestyle:

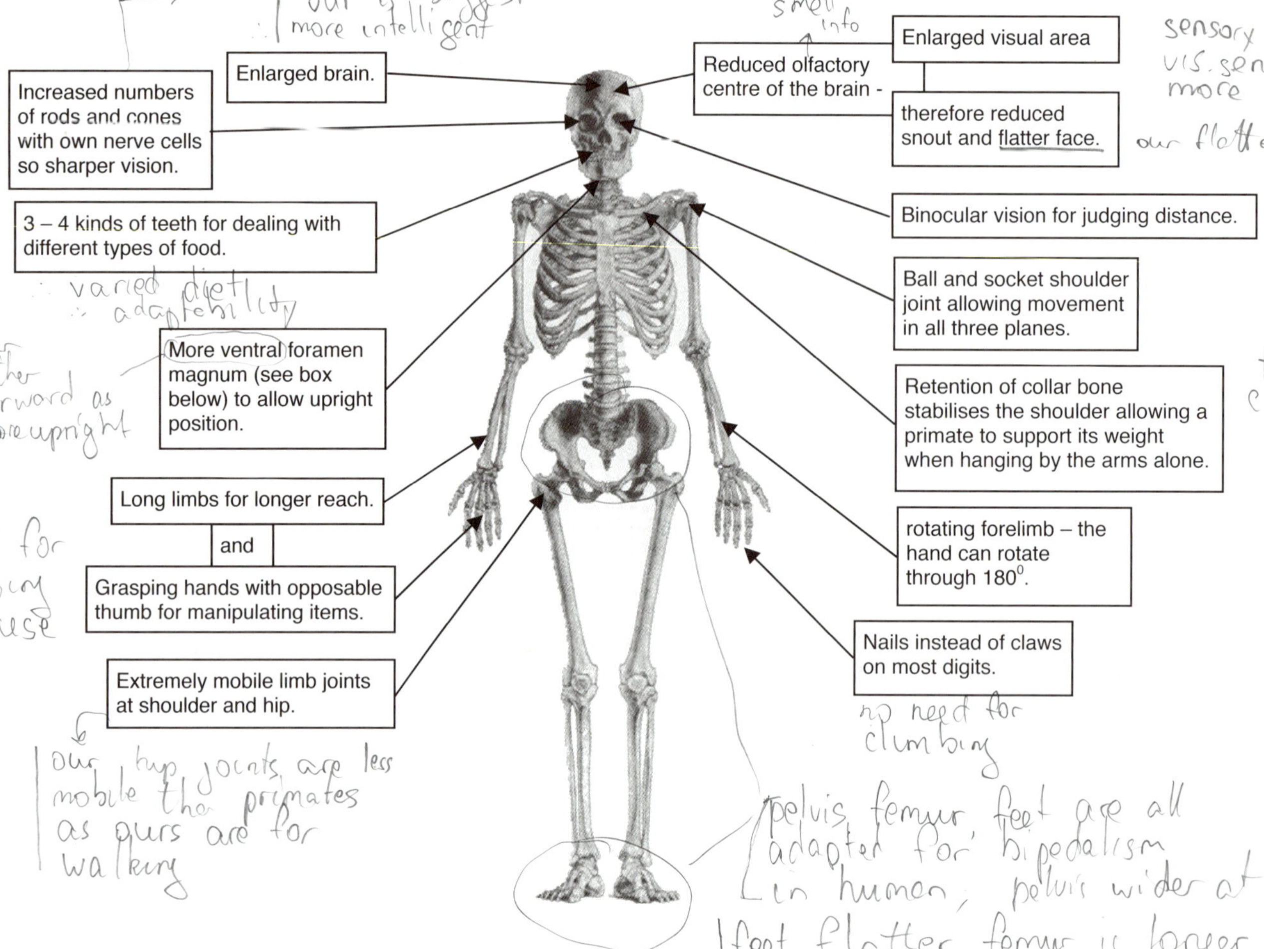

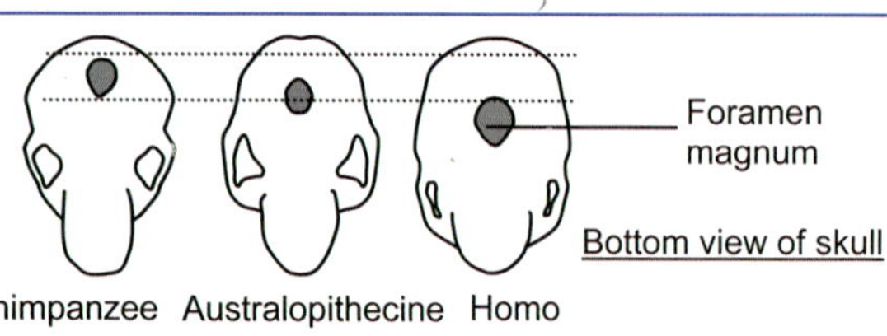

Note how the foramen magnum has moved to a more central position where the skull is balanced more centrally indicating a move from quadrupedal to bipedal habit.

At various stages in hominid evolution several species may have coexisted – example *H. neanderthalensis* and *H. sapiens.*

mya = millions of years ago

Trends in the Human Fossils

Ardipithecus ramidus

- Few fossil remains found so description uncertain;
- Ape-like dentition but transitional between apes and Australopithecines;
- Tooth enamel very thin compared to hominids;
- Hominid type canines – low and blunt;
- Incisors larger than hominids but smaller than chimpanzees;
- more centrally positioned foramen magnum indicating a trend towards bipedalism. (See box on previous page).

4.4 – 4.3mya;
Height possibly slightly smaller than *afarensis*;
East Africa.

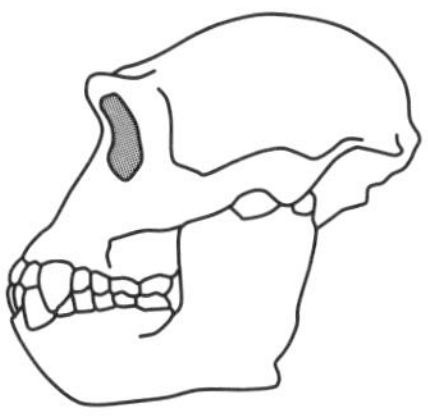

Australopithecus afarensis

- ape-like face;
- flat nose;
- no chin;
- protruding jaws;
- canines smaller than modern apes;
- large molars;
- males much larger than females.

3.9 – 2.5mya;
height 1.07 – 1.52m;
brain size 375 – 550cm^3;
East Africa.

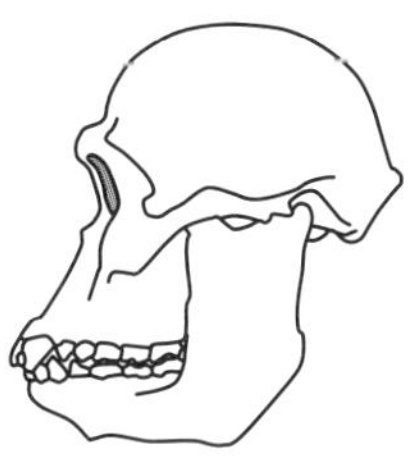

Australopithecus africanus

- flatter face;
- smaller canines;
- larger molars.

3.0 – 2.3mya;
height 1.1 – 1.4m;
brain size 420 - 500cm^3;
Southern Africa.

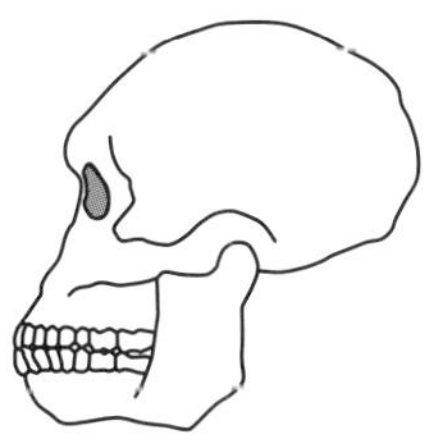

Homo habilis

- smaller teeth and jaws;
- this indicates more meat in the diet;
- first to adapt and use stone tools;
- hips form a distinct pelvic bowl;
- near to modern humans in size;
- males and females similar size.

2.4 – 1.6mya;
height 1.0 – 1.5m;
brain size 500 - 800cm^3;
Eastern / Southern Africa.

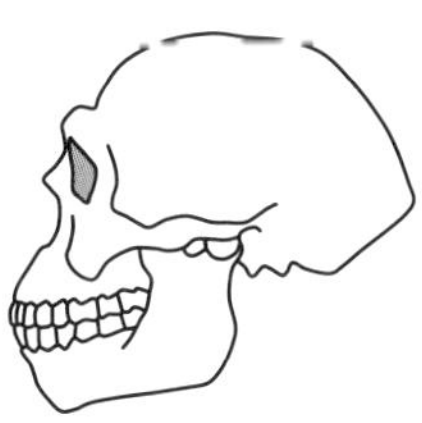

Homo erectus

- meat formed a significant part of their diet;
- rib-cage barrel-shaped;
- sophisticated stone-tool makers;
- probably used fire.

1.8 – 0.3mya;
height 1.3 – 1.5m;
brain size 750 – 1225cm^3;
Africa, Indonesia, Asia.

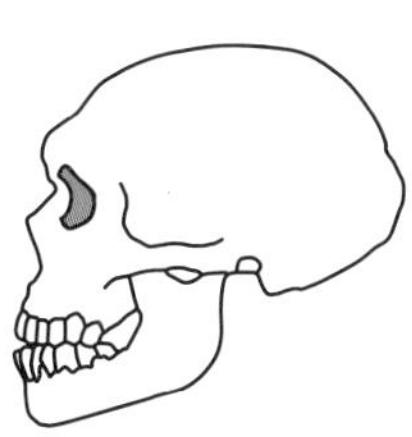

Homo neanderthalensis

- large-brained;
- heavy-boned;
- large teeth and jaw muscles;
- brow-ridge above the eye sockets was nearly as prominent as in *H. erectus*;
- limbs were relatively short with respect to the torso (indicating an adaptation to the cold).

150,000 – 30,000 years ago;
height 1.5 – 1.7m;
brain size 1200 - 1625cm^3;
Europe, western Asia.

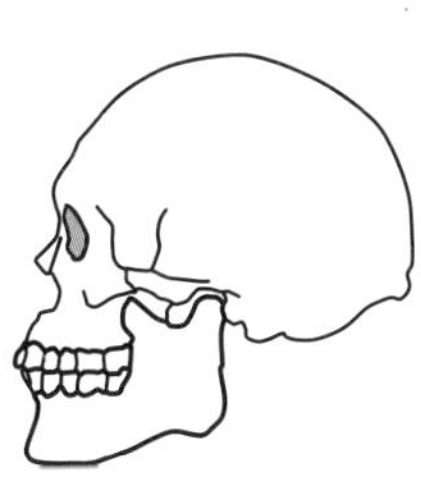

Homo sapiens sapiens

- large brain;
- face flat rather than projecting;
- molars and canines reduced in size;
- brow-ridge reduced;
- lower jaw is reinforced on the outside producing a chin – this is absent from other hominids;
- general trend towards smaller molars and reduced robustness.

130,000 years ago to present;
height 1.6 – 1.8m;
brain size 1200 - 1500cm^3;
Africa and western Asia.

The Fossil Record

Key points

- Understanding of human evolution is based mainly on the fossil record;
- The fossil record is very data-poor;
- Fossilisation is a rare event;
- Only bones and teeth as the hard parts are likely to become fossilised;
- Fossilisation less likely in wet areas as organic acids from vegetation dissolve the calcium salts in bones and teeth;
- Most fossils have therefore come from dry regions;
- Discovering a fossil is a rare event;
- The fossils found are often only fragments, especially the earlier ones;
- The time spans involved are very large and forming links from one fossil group to another involves various levels of speculation;
- New discoveries can often cause major changes in the theories.

Diet and Brain Size

Points for Discussion

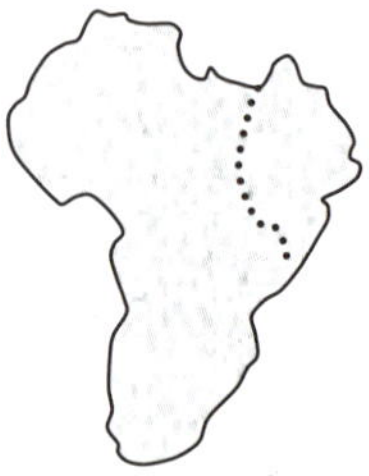

- Between 5 and 1.8 million years ago, besides there being a continued cooling and drying of the global climate, the shifting of the Earth's tectonic plates caused a vast rift to form in Eastern Africa (shown as on the map) in the area where many hominids were soon to be found: the Rift Valley;
- The effect was to drastically alter water-courses and to push up mountain ranges which, in turn, altered the weather patterns;
- More rain fell on the west of the Rift (which helped maintain rainforest) and the eastern part became progressively drier;
- In these dry conditions, forested areas dwindled and were replaced by open, grassy plains and scattered trees;
- Food availability is obviously crucial to survival;
- With fewer trees, and hence less fruit and tender leaves, apes in the east at this time could move west, adapt to a new diet, or go extinct;
- The changes seen in the jaws and teeth of the Australopithecines indicate that they adapted to eating tougher types of vegetation such as stems, tubers and roots;

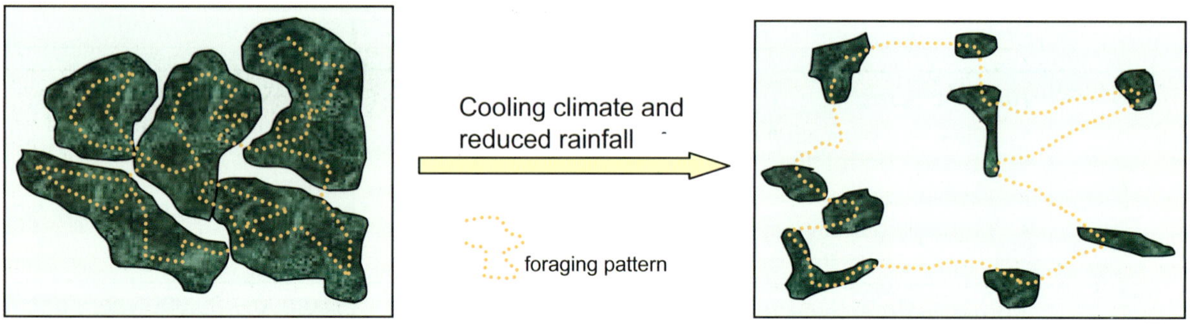

- Near continuous forest;
- Food sources abundant;
- For pre-hominids a tree-dwelling life was possible almost all the time.

- Wooded savannah;
- Food sources diminished;
- Pre-hominids forced to spend more time on the ground;
- Experimentation with different food sources.

- The greater availability and accessibility of grazing animals on the grassy plains may have stimulated an adaptation to eating more meat, possibly at first by scavenging and then by hunting and killing;
- The need to develop hunting strategies and to discover novel, hard-to-get, and more nutritious food such as insect grubs, would have driven a selection for larger and more intelligent brains;
- The brain consumes a lot of energy;
- Diets rich in protein and energy containing fat would have allowed development of the larger brain.

Genetic Evolution

- This is the change in the genotype of the population resulting in speciation;
- The time periods are measured in millions of years.

Cultural Evolution

- This is the process by which knowledge and traditions are passed on from one generation to the next by teaching and observation.

Points for discussion

- Hominids have large brains capable of reasoning and learning;
- New skills can be developed;
  - hunting;
  - tool making;
  - farming;
  - building;
  - medicine;
  - science;
  - art;
  - politics;
  - customs;
  - law;
  - religion.
- The skills can be refined, modified, added to;
- These can be passed on through language and writing so they do not have to be repeatedly discovered;
- To use language it is clear that genetic factors are important –
  - to cause the development of the voice-box;
  - develop the parts of the brain devoted to forming sounds;
  - the brain-power to manipulate symbols rapidly.
- However, once we have language, then the symbols and ideas that are exchanged between individuals, groups, and cultures are free from genetic influence and any changes can all be said to be due to cultural evolution;
- This evolution of culture can be very rapid compared to genetic evolution;
- Cultural differences can lead to subdivisions into different groups;
- Or different genetic groups could develop different cultures;
- In turn this has lead to conflict between different cultural groups.

Define half-life.

Using potassium-argon dating how many half lives have passed if there are equal numbers of potassium and argon atoms?

What is the half life of ^{14}C?

What is the half life of ^{40}K?

List five physical features that define humans as primates.

State the approximate dates of –	State the distribution of –
Ardipithecus ramidus -	*Ardipithecus ramidus* -
Australopithecus afarensis -	*Australopithecus afarensis* -
A. africanus -	*A. africanus* -
Homo habilis -	*Homo habilis* -
H. erectus -	*H. erectus* -
H. neanderthalensis -	*H. neanderthalensis* -
H. sapiens -	*H. sapiens* -

State two comparative features for each of the following –

Ardipithecus ramidus -

Australopithecus afarensis -

A. africanus -

Homo habilis -

H. erectus -

H. neanderthalensis -

H. sapiens -

List 7 points that can be used in a discussion on the incompleteness of the fossil record and uncertainties about human evolution.

List 7 points that can be used in a discussion on the correlation between diet and brain size during hominid evolution.

State the difference between cultural and genetic evolution.

Describe three features of cultural evolution.

Extension material – HL only

❖ The Hardy-Weinberg Principle

Adaptation and Allele Frequency

- If a particular adaptation depends on *genetic* information, then it is possible to count its 'success' or 'failure' in terms of the proportion of the gene's alleles found in the population's gene pool;
- Thus, if a gene has two alleles, it may well be that one of them confers more chances of survival and reproduction than the other does;
- In this case, the frequency of the 'successful' allele in the gene pool will tend to increase at the expense of the 'less successful'.

Deriving the Hardy-Weinberg Equation

Key steps

- The population size is always considered as 1;
- The dominant allele A has a frequency p in the population;
- The recessive allele a has a frequency q in the population;
- The *maximum* frequency of an allele in a gene pool is 1 (equivalent to 100%) and the minimum is 0. (See p8).
- For the two alleles, *p* and *q*, their frequency when added together must equal 1;
  - With only 2 alleles, if, say, 60% of the alleles in the pool are of the *p* type, the other 40% *must* be the *q* type – remember the population size is always 1;
- Therefore p + q = 1;
- Assuming fertilisation is random –
  - a sperm with a p allele has an equal chance of fusing with an egg with a p allele or an egg with a q allele;
  - a sperm with a q allele has an equal chance of fusing with an egg with a p allele or an egg with a q allele;
- Putting these into a Punnett grid we get -

eggs \ sperms	p	q
p	p^2	pq
q	pq	q^2

- The sum of these chances must add up to the total population size of 1;
- Hence we get the Hardy-Weinberg equation -

$$p^2 + 2pq + q^2 = 1$$

The Hardy-Weinberg Principle states that if the frequency of one allele, A, is p, and the frequency of the other allele, a, is q, then the frequency of the genotype –

- AA is p^2
- Aa is 2pq
- aa is q^2.

Conditions for the Hardy-Weinberg principle.

- Large population;
- Random mating;
- Constant allele frequency over time;
- No mutation;
- No immigration or emigration;
- No allele-specific mortality.

Calculating Allele, Genotype and Phenotype Frequencies

Key points

- If the frequency of one allele is known the frequency of the other can be calculated using the equation $p + q = 1$;
- If the frequency of the recessive phenotype is known then the frequencies of the homozygous dominant and heterozygous genotypes can be calculated using the Hardy-Weinberg equation.

Worked examples

Problem 1

- If the frequency of $p = 0.79$ what is the frequency of q?
  - The frequency of $q = 1 - 0.79 = 0.21$.

Problem 2

- If one individual in a population of 10,000 shows the recessive phenotype what are the frequencies of the dominant and recessive alleles?
  - 1 in 10,000 is the same as 0.0001 in a population of 1;
  - The frequency of the recessive phenotype is q^2;
  - Therefore $q^2 = 0.0001$;
  - Therefore the frequency of the recessive allele $q = 0.01$;
  - Therefore the frequency of the dominant allele $p = 1 - 0.01 = 0.99$.

There are 3 problems on Hardy-Weinberg in Appendix 1 on pages 28-29, and the answers are in Appendix 2 on page 30.

Problem 3

- If the frequency of $q^2 = 0.0049$ what is the frequency of 2pq?
  - If $q^2 = 0.0049$, $q = 0.07$;
  - Therefore $p = 1 – 0.07 = 0.93$;
  - Therefore $2pq = 2 \times 0.07 \times 0.93 = 0.1302$.

Problem 4

- In a particular plant species the allele R for round pollen grains is dominant to the allele r for long pollen grains. In a population of 200 plants, 32 have long pollen grains. Determine how many plants are like to be heterozygous.
  - 32 in a population of 200 is the same as 0.16 in a population of 1 ($32 \div 200$);
  - Plants with long pollen grains are the homozygous recessive and have the genotype rr;
  - Therefore $q^2 = 0.16$ and $q = 0.4$;
  - Therefore $p = 0.6$;
  - Therefore $2pq = 0.48$ in a population of 1;
  - Therefore 96 plants in the population of 200 are heterozygous.

State the Hardy-Weinberg equation.

List the conditions under which the Hardy-Weinberg principle applies.

Show how the Hardy-Weinberg equation is derived.

❖ Phylogeny and Systematics

The Value of Classifying Organisms – a Natural Classification

Key reasons

- Organisation - allows order rather than randomness (imagine supermarket shelves arranged randomly!) and hence easier identification.
- Naming – common names vary from place to place whereas the scientific binomial name is consistent throughout the world.
- Prediction of characteristics – it is easy to remember groups of common features and hence be able to predict the presence of others.
- Evolutionary relationships – shared characteristics probably means a common origin, indicating evolutionary pathways.

Homologous Characteristics (See page 10)
Ones that share a common evolutionary origin but do not necessarily have the same function now.
Examples –
- bird wing and bat wing;
- human arm and horse front leg;
- whale flipper and chimpanzee arm.

Analogous Characteristics (See page 11)
Ones which now have a similar function but different evolutionary origins.
Examples –
- bird wing and butterfly wing;
- wasp eye and octopus eye;
- beetle leg and cat leg.

The Universality of DNA and Protein Structure

Key points

- All organisms use DNA as their genetic material;
- All organisms use the same genetic code, ie the mRNA codon table;
- All proteins are made from the same 20 amino acids;
- All amino acids used in proteins are of the L form;
- These four facts strongly indicate a common ancestry.

Some viruses use RNA as their genetic material, but since they are non-living they are not classed as organisms.

In the laboratory there are two forms of all but one of the amino acids, the L form and the D form. In Urey and Miller's experiment both forms of amino acid appeared in the 'soup'.

Molecular Variation and Phylogeny

Phylogeny is the evolutionary history of a group of organisms which will therefore have genetic linkages between ancestors and descendants.

Key points

- Molecules of organisms are heritable characteristics;
- Variation in their structure will be a consequence of variation in the genes that produce them;
- Proteins give relatively precise information about phylogenies;
- Genetic differences between taxa are estimated by obtaining homologous proteins from them and determining the number of changes in amino acid sequence;
- DNA analysis of flightless birds shows that, although kiwis and moas (a giant and extinct flightless bird) lived together in New Zealand, they were not closely related.

The molecular phylogeny of flightless birds

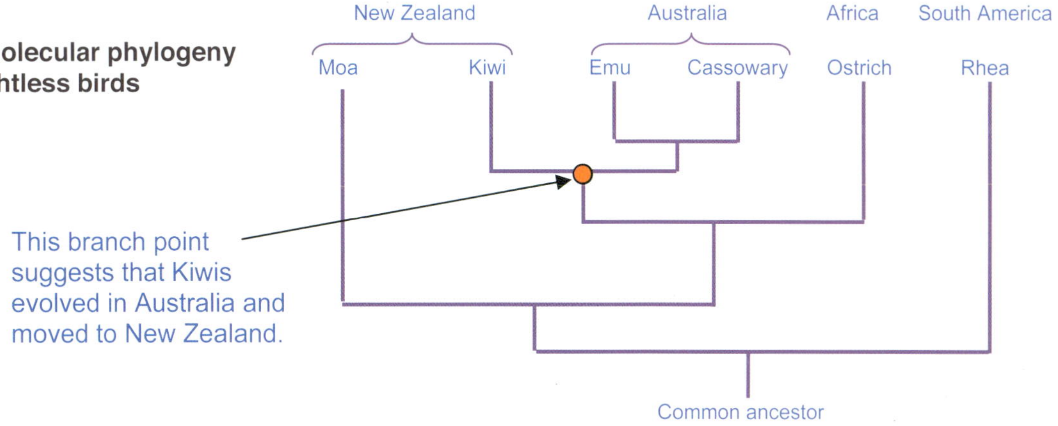

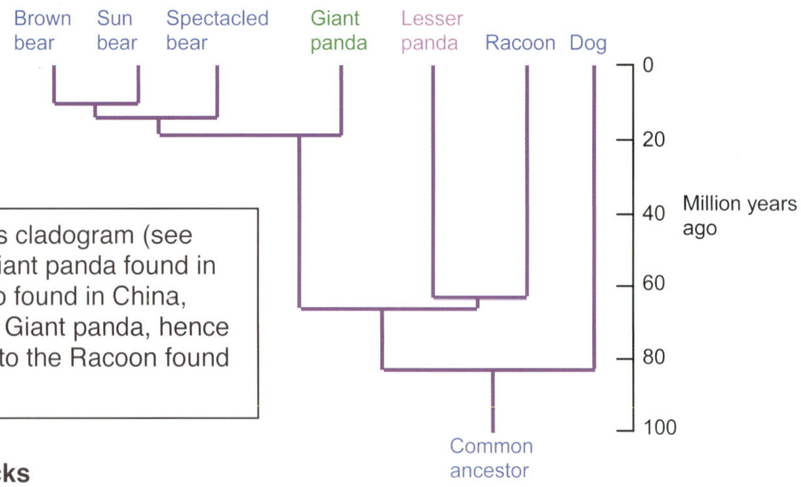

DNA analysis was used to construct this cladogram (see next section) and has shown that the Giant panda found in China is a bear. The Lesser panda, also found in China, was thought to be closely related to the Giant panda, hence its name, but in fact it is closely related to the Racoon found in America.

Molecular Variation and Evolutionary Clocks

Points for discussion

- Changes (mutations) in the DNA base sequence can accumulate in the genome over time, provided they do not affect survival;
- There is evidence that these changes show a roughly constant rate of change, ie act as a molecular clock;
- DNA is a very stable molecule and therefore fossil DNA can be analysed;
- DNA is easy to sequence;
- Changes in the DNA base sequence will also result in a corresponding change in the amino acid sequence of the polypeptide;
- Thus the greater the number of differences between the amino acid sequences of the same polypeptide in different organisms indicates a more distance common ancestor;
- DNA accumulates more changes than the corresponding polypeptide which increases the accuracy of the molecular clock, eg. - introns can change without affecting the final polypeptide;
  - a codon can change without affecting the final amino acid at that position;
- Mitochondrial and chloroplast DNA can also be used to run in parallel with nuclear DNA analysis.

Clades, Cladistics and Cladograms

Clade
All of the organisms, both living and fossil, descended from a particular common ancestor.

Cladistics
A method of classifying living organisms based on the construction and analysis of cladograms.

- A cladogram is an evolutionary tree showing points at which lineages diverged from a common ancestral form.
- It can use biochemical data, eg number of differences in DNA base or amino acid sequences, or morphological data, ie characteristics.

Constructing a Cladogram using Biochemical Data

The syllabus states that either morphological or biochemical data can be used to construct a cladogram. I would though advise you to learn both methods as examiners have been known to make mistakes and not give you the choice!

Biochemical data could be given in different ways.

Example 1
The table shows the number of amino acid differences between the human hemoglobin beta chain and a number of other animals.

human	horse	grey kangaroo	cow	gorilla	rhesus monkey
0	25	38	25	1	8

Rearrange the data into descending order.

grey kangaroo	horse	cow	rhesus monkey	gorilla	human
38	25	25	8	1	0

Assuming that the rate of change is constant a cladogram can be drawn to scale.

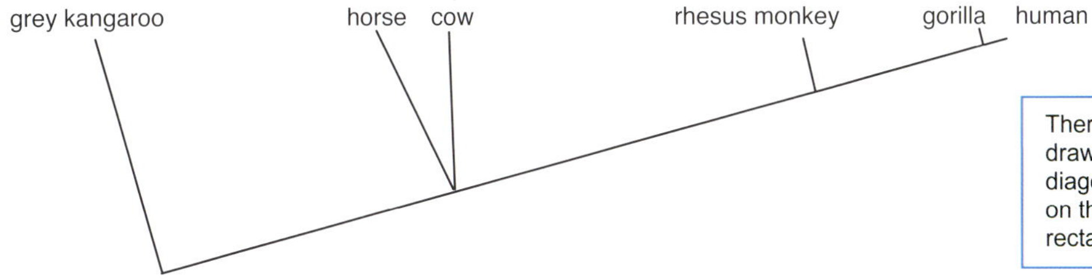

There are various ways of drawing a cladogram. This is the diagonal branch form. The one on the next page is the rectangular branch form.

Example 2

The table below shows the nucleotide differences in the genes coding for cytochrome c, a compound used in aerobic respiration. The organisms are in random order.

	human	dog	horse	monkey	donkey
human					
dog	13				
horse	17	10			
monkey	1	12	16		
donkey	16	8	1	15	
pig	13	4	5	12	4

We now need to re-arrange the data so that the number of differences decreases across each row.
The first one is simple as there is only 1 difference between the human and monkey.
Now look for the smallest number. This is the 1 difference between horse and donkey, so add these along with the differences with human and monkey. Note that the order in which the organisms are listed in the top row (left to right), must be the same as in the first column (from top to bottom).

	human	monkey	horse	donkey	
human					
monkey	1				
horse	17	16			
donkey	16	15	1		

Now find the next smallest. This is pig / dog and pig / donkey. Donkey is already in the table.

	human	monkey	horse	donkey	dog
human					
monkey	1				
horse	17	16			
donkey	16	15	1		
dog	13	12	10	8	
pig	13	12	5	4	4

We can see that there are 8 differences between a dog and donkey but only 4 differences between a pig and a donkey, so pigs are closer to donkeys. We need to swap them over in the table.

	human	monkey	horse	donkey	pig
human					
monkey	1				
horse	17	16			
donkey	16	15	1		
pig	13	12	5	4	
dog	13	12	10	8	4

We can now draw the cladogram. The human and monkey only differ by 1 as do the horse and donkey. Therefore these pairs must be joined at nodes. The pig and the dog do not differ much and so should be joined at a node. However the pig is more closely related to the horse and donkey than the dog and so needs to be joined at a node closer to the horse and donkey.

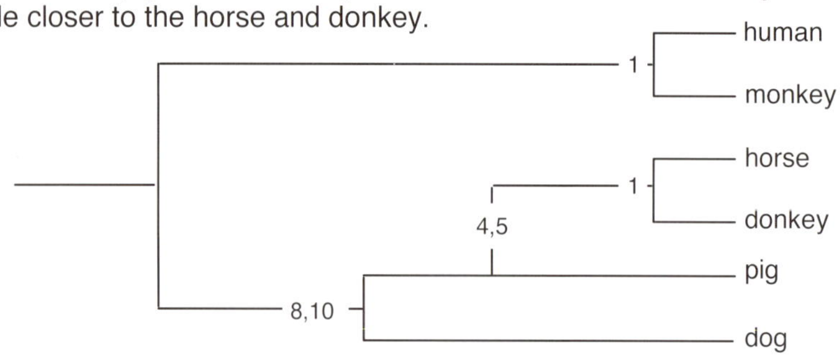

This is not totally accurate as all 6 organisms are brought back to a single node. There are fewer differences between human/monkey and horse/donkey than there are when comparing human/monkey with pig/dog. Consequently there should be another node separating pigs from dogs which the data does not allow us to currently draw.
There is a problem in Appendix 3 on page 31 for you to try and the answer is in Appendix 4 on page 36.

Constructing a Cladogram using Morphological Data

Key steps

> Don't worry if you do not know what a particular characteristic is. All that matters is whether the organism has it or not.

1. Draw up a table of the characteristics and organisms you have chosen. Put a + in the box if the organism has the characteristics and a – if it does not.

Character	Organism			
	Frog	Duck	Bat	Anteater
1. Hair	-	-	+	+
2. Mammary glands	-	-	+	+
3. Wings.	-	+	+	-
4. Fingers and toes	+	+	+	+
5. Sticky tongue	+	-	-	+
6. 3 ear bones	-	-	+	+
7. Spiral cochlea	-	-	+	+
8. Endothermy	-	+	+	+
9. Amnion	-	+	+	+
10. Diaphragm	-	+	+	+
11. Placenta	-	-	+	+
12. Internal fertilisation	-	+	+	+

2. Reorganise the table with decreasing numbers of shared + boxes. It does not matter in which order you put the rows with equal numbers of + boxes. The four rows below with 3 + boxes I have simply put in numerical order 8, 9, 10, 12, but it would make no difference if I put them as 10, 12, 8, 9.

Characteristic	Organism			
	Frog	Duck	Bat	Anteater
4. Fingers and toes	+	+	+	+
8. Endothermy	-	+	+	+
9. Amnion	-	+	+	+
10. Diaphragm	-	+	+	+
12. Internal fertilisation	-	+	+	+
1. Hair	-	-	+	+
2. Mammary glands	-	-	+	+
6. 3 ear bones	-	-	+	+
7. Spiral cochlea	-	-	+	+
11. Placenta	-	-	+	+
3. Wings.	-	+	+	-
5. Sticky tongue	+	-	-	+

3. Now we can draw the cladogram.

- 4 must be the common ancestral characteristic as all four organisms possess it so it goes at the base.
- The next branch point must be characteristics 8, 9, 10 and 12 as these are shared by 3 of the organisms.
- The next branch point must be characteristics 1, 2, 6, 7 and 11 as these are shared by two of the organisms.
- This leaves characteristics 3 and 5. 3 is a characteristic that has probably evolved independently as a result of convergent evolution. 5 is probably the same but the anteater is the only one in this cladogram to show it.

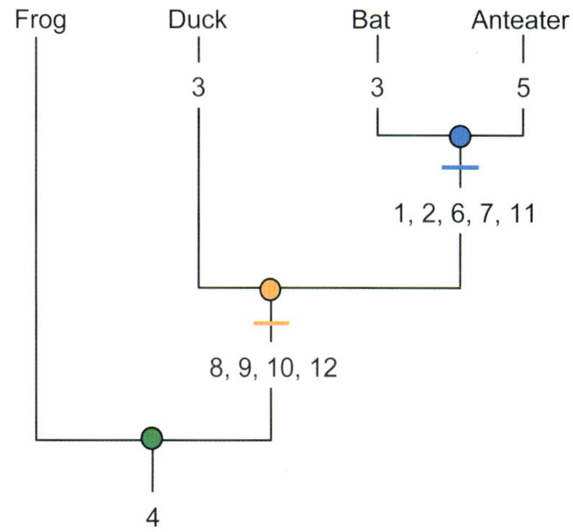

There are four more examples in Appendix 3 on pages 32 to 35 for you to practise on and the answers are in Appendix 4 on pages 37 to 41.

Cladogram Terms

Look at the cladogram above.
- ➢ The coloured circles where the tree branches are called **nodes**;
- ➢ Groups of organisms that share a common ancestor form a **clade**;
- ➢ This is easily seen with the 'snip rule';
- ➢ The bat and anteater form a clade if you snip at the blue line;
- ➢ The duck, bat and anteater form a clade if you snip at the orange line;
- ➢ The duck and bat do not form a clade because snipping at the orange line means the anteater falls off as well and must therefore be included;
- ➢ The length of the branches in morphological cladograms is arbitrary and does not show evolutionary distances;
- ➢ The length of the branches in biochemical cladograms sometimes shows evolutionary distances based on the number of changes;

Using a Cladogram to show Phylogenetic Relationships

Key points

Look again at the cladogram above.
- ➢ All four organisms share the ancestral characteristic, fingers and toes;
- ➢ At the green node 4 new characteristics appear that are shared by the duck, bat and anteater but not by the frog;
- ➢ At the orange node 5 new characteristics appear that are shared by the bat and anteater but not by the duck;
- ➢ At the orange node the duck develops wings which is not shared by the bat or the anteater;
- ➢ At the blue node the bat develops wings and the anteater a sticky tongue;
- ➢ Development of wings is a convergent characteristic;
- ➢ Many other characteristics could have been used, eg characteristic 4, fingers and toes, could have been replaced with lungs;

Cladograms and Classification

Points for discussion
- ➢ The phylogenetic trees produced by cladograms can be compared to the ones used by other methods such as fossils;
- ➢ In most cases they will agree because they use the same principles – evolutionary relationships;
- ➢ Depending on which characteristics are used means the nodes can occur at different places, which may cause some confusion;
- ➢ In some cases a particular morphology based cladogram differs from the traditional classification. This can often be resolved using a molecular cladogram. An example is the Giant and Lesser pandas shown above;
- ➢ However the molecular clock may not 'tick' at a constant rate resulting in inaccurate positioning of nodes.

Appendix 1 – Hardy-Weinberg problems

Problem 1

Ear lobes in humans can be either attached or unattached. The allele for free ear lobes, F, is dominant over the allele, f, for attached ear lobes. Suppose that in a population of 10,000 there are 8400 people who have free ear lobes. Calculate the allele frequency and also the proportion of people with each of the three genotypes.

Problem 2

Cystic fibrosis, a recessive genetic mutation, occurs in some populations with a frequency of 1 in 2000. Calculate the frequency of the heterozygote.

Problem 3

A population of flour beetles contains 64 with brown wings and 36 with black wings. (Black wings is recessive). What proportion of the brown winged beetles are homozygous and what proportion are heterozygous?

Appendix 2 – Answers to Hardy-Weinberg problems

Problem 1

Ear lobes in humans can be either attached or unattached. The allele for free ear lobes, F, is dominant over the allele, f, for attached ear lobes. Suppose that in a population of 10,000 there are 8400 people who have free ear lobes. Calculate the allele frequency and also the proportion of people with each of the three genotypes.

Since free ear lobes is dominant the 8400 people are a mixture of homozygous and heterozygous. The remaining 1600 are homozygous recessive, ff. Thus in a population of 1 there are 1600 ÷ 10,000 = 0.16 individuals that are homozygous recessive.
Therefore $q^2 = 0.16$;
Therefore $q = 0.4$;
Therefore $p = 0.6$;
Therefore $p^2 = 0.36$
and $2pq = 0.48$;
Therefore the population of 10,000 is made up of –
- 3600 homozygous dominant FF, [p^2]
- 4800 heterozygous Ff, [2pq],
- 1600 homozygous recessive, ff, [q^2].

$$p^2 + 2pq + q^2 = 1$$
$$0.36 + 0.48 + 0.16 = 1$$

Problem 2

Cystic fibrosis, a recessive genetic mutation, occurs in some populations with a frequency of 1 in 2000. Calculate the frequency of the heterozygote.

Since cystic fibrosis is recessive the frequency of 1 in 2000 is q^2.
Therefore $q^2 = 0.0005$.
Therefore $q = 0.0224$.
Therefore $p = 1 - 0.0224 = 0.9776$.
Therefore $2pq = 2 \times 0.9776 \times 0.0224$
$= 0.044$ or 4.4 in 100.
Or 4.4%.

Problem 3

A population of flour beetles contains 64 with brown wings and 36 with black wings. (Black wings is recessive).
What proportion of the brown winged beetles are homozygous and what proportion are heterozygous?

The total population is 64 + 36 = 100.
36 beetles have the recessive black wing.
Therefore q^2 = 36 in 100 = 0.36.
Therefore $q = 0.6$.
Therefore $p = 1 - 0.6 = 0.4$.
Therefore $p^2 = 0.16$.
Therefore 16 in the population are homozygous.
$2pq = 2 \times 0.4 \times 0.6 = 0.48$.
Therefore 48 in the population are heterozygous.
Check : 16 + 48 = 64.

Appendix 3 – Cladogram problems

Constructing a cladogram from biochemical data

The table shows part of the amino acid sequence of cytochrome c of 5 organisms. The shaded boxes are where there is the same amino acid as a human.

	1				5					10					15					20
human	Asp	Val	Glu	Lys	Gly	Lys	Lys	Ile	Phe	Ile	Met	Lys	Cys	Ser	Gln	Cys	Thr	Val	Glu	Lys
yeast	Ser	Ala	Lys			Ala	Thr	Leu		Lys	Thr	Arg		Glu	Leu					
chicken		Ile								Val	Gln									Glu
pig								Asn		Val	Gln			Arg						
dogfish		Met						Val		Val	Gln			Ala						Asn

Scan along pairs of organisms and count the number of differences. Here are some blank tables to help you.

	human	yeast	chicken	pig	dogfish
human					
yeast	11				
chicken	4	12			
pig	4	11	4		
dogfish	6	12		4	

	human	pig	chicken	dogfish	
human					
pig	4				
chicken	4	4			
dogfish	6	4	4		
yeast	11	11	11	12	

Now you can build your cladogram.

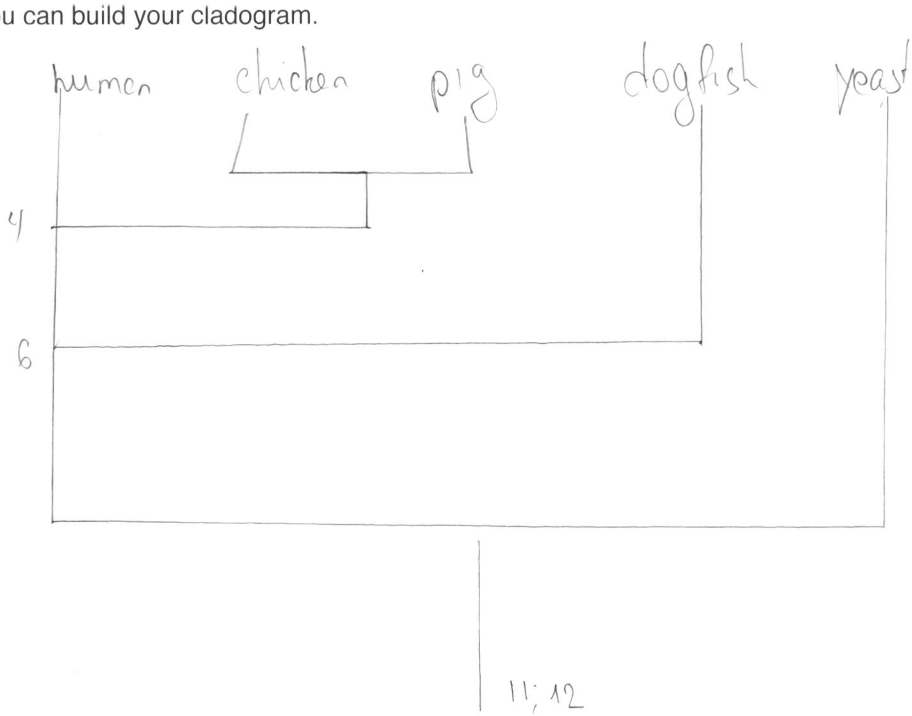

Constructing a cladogram from morphological data

Problem 1

Characteristic	Organism			
	fern	moss	daisy	tulip
1. Photosynthetic gametophyte	+	+	-	-
2. Dispersal by seeds	-	-	+	+
3. Chlorophyll	+	+	+	+
4. Dispersal by spores	+	+	-	-
5. Vascular tissue	+	-	+	+
6. Flowers	-	-	+	+
7. Dominant sporophyte	+	-	+	+
8. True roots	+	-	+	+

Step 1 Re-organise the rows so that there is a decreasing number of + symbols in each row. Don't worry if you don't know what a photosynthetic gametophyte is – it is the + and – symbols that matter, not the actual characteristics.

Characteristic	Organism			
	Moss	daisy	tulip	fern
3 Chlorophyll	+	+	+	+
8 True roots	–	+	+	+
7 Dom. sporophyte	–	+	+	+
5 Vascular tissue	–	+	+	+
4 Disp by spores	+	–	–	+
2 Disp by seeds	–	+	+	–
6 Flowers	–	+	+	–
1 Ph. gametophyte	+	–	–	+

Here are further blank tables if you need to do some reorganising.

Characteristic	Organism			

Characteristic	Organism			

Now you can build your cladogram.

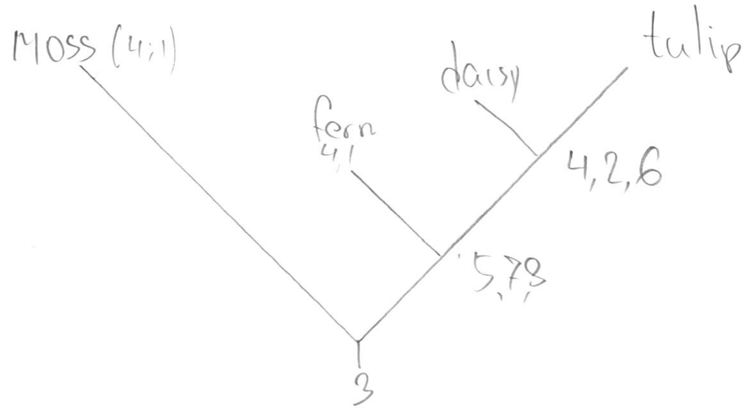

Problem 2

Characteristic	Organism						
	lizard	Orangutan	lamprey	bear	sunfish	Amphioxus	newt
1. jaws	+	+	-	+	+	-	+
2. mammary glands	-	+	-	+	-	-	-
3. opposable thumbs	-	+	-	-	-	-	-
4. amniotic egg	+	+	-	+	-	-	-
5. backbone	+	+	+	+	+	-	+
6. four limbs	+	+	-	+	-	-	+

Steps 1 and 2 Reorganise the rows and columns in order to produce a decreasing number of + symbols going both down and left to right. Do the rows first, then the columns.

Characteristic	Organism						
	Amphiox	lamprey	Sunfish	Newt	lizard	bear	Or.
5 backbone	–	+	+	+	+	+	+
1 Mammaly glands	–	–	+	+	+	+	+
6 4 limbs	–	–	–	+	+	+	+
4 Am. egg	–	–	–	–	+	+	+
2 Mammary glands	–	–	–	–	–	+	+
3 Opp thums	–	–	–	–	–	–	+

Characteristic	Organism						

Now you can build your cladogram.

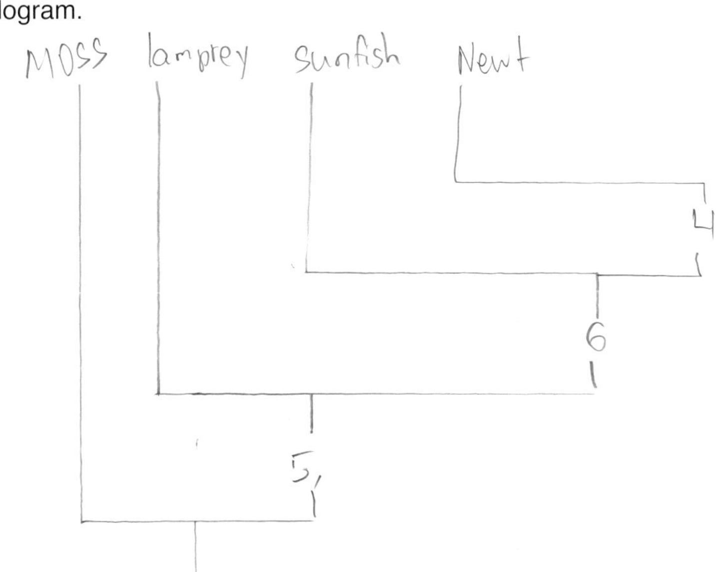

Problem 3

Characteristic	Organism							
	salamander	chimpanzee	perch	mouse	lizard	pigeon	hagfish	
1. Feathers	-	-	-	-	-	+	-	1
2. Fur	-	+	-	+	-	-	-	2
3. Mammary glands	-	+	-	+	-	-	-	2
4. Lungs	+	+	-	+	+	+	-	5
5. Claws or nails	-	+	-	+	+	+	-	4
6. Jaws	+	+	+	+	+	+	-	6
	2	5	1	5	3	4	0	

Characteristic	Organism						
	hagfish	perch	salamand	lizard	pigeon	mouse	chimp
Jaws	−	+	+	+	+	+	+
lungs	−	−	+	+	+	+	+
Claws	−	−	−	+	+	+	+
Fur	−	−	−	−	−	+	+
Mammary glands	−		−	−	−	+	+
Feathers	−	−	−	−	+	−	−

Characteristic	Organism						

Now you can build your cladogram.

Problem 4

Characteristic	Organism							
	sharks	ray-finned fish	primates	rodents	crocodiles	birds	amphibians	
1. 2 post-orbital fenestrae	-	-	-	-	+	+	-	2
2. vertebrae	+	+	+	+	+	+	+	6
3. four limbs	-	-	+	+	+	+	+	4
4. amniotic egg	-	-	+	+	+	+	-	3
5. hair	-	-	+	+	-	-	-	2
6. bony skeleton	-	+	+	+	+	+	+	5
	1	2	5	5	5	5	3	

Characteristic	Organism						
	Sharks	r.f.f.	amph.	crocodiles	birds	primates	rodents
vertebrae	+	+	+	+	+	+	+
bony skeleton	–	+	+	+	+	+	+
4 limbs	–	–	+	+	+	+	+
amn egg	–	–	–	+	+	+	+
hair	–	–	-	–	–	+	[illegible]
2 post orb f	–	–	–	+	+	–	–

Characteristic	Organism						

Now you can build your cladogram.

Appendix 4 – Answers to the cladogram problems

Constructing a cladogram from biochemical data
The table shows part of the amino acid sequence of cytochrome c of 5 organisms. The shaded boxes are where there is the same amino acid as a human.

	1				5					10					15					20
human	Asp	Val	Glu	Lys	Gly	Lys	Lys	Ile	Phe	Ile	Met	Lys	Cys	Ser	Gln	Cys	Thr	Val	Glu	Lys
yeast	Ser	Ala	Lys			Ala	Thr	Leu		Lys	Thr	Arg		Glu	Leu					
chicken		Ile								Val	Gln									Glu
pig								Asn		Val	Gln			Arg						
dogfish		Met						Val		Val	Gln			Ala						Asn

Scan along pairs of organisms and count the number of differences.

	human	yeast	chicken	pig
human				
yeast	11			
chicken	4	12		
pig	4	11	4	
dogfish	6	12	4	4

Yeast has the greatest number of differences with all the organisms and so must go on the bottom.
The dogfish has the next greatest difference with a human and therefore should be the second to bottom row.
The pig and chicken have the least number of differences with a human. It does not matter which way round because both will come off at the same node.

	human	pig	chicken	dogfish
human				
pig	4			
chicken	4	4		
dogfish	6	4	4	
yeast	11	11	12	12

We can now construct the cladogram. Since yeast differs by the nearly the same number from the other 4 then it should be on a line of its own. The dogfish has a node at 6 and the chicken and pig have a node at 4.

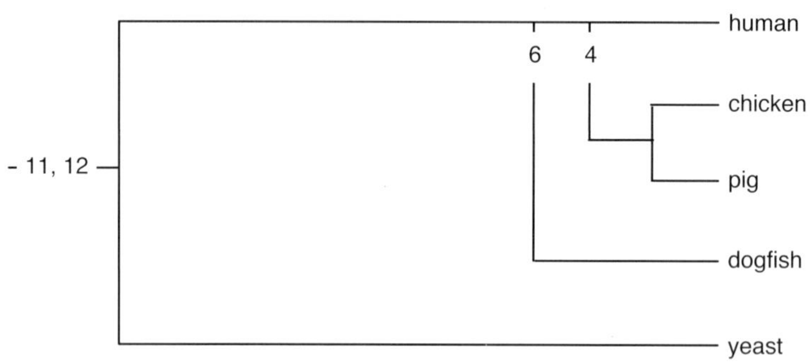

Since you 'know' that a pig and human are more closely related than a chicken and human you may want to swap chicken and pig over. However, simply based on the data given either cladogram is correct.

Constructing a cladogram from morphological data

Problem 1

Characteristic	Organism			
	fern	moss	daisy	tulip
1. Photosynthetic gametophyte	+	+	-	-
2. Dispersal by seeds	-	-	+	+
3. Chlorophyll	+	+	+	+
4. Dispersal by spores	+		-	-
5. Vascular tissue	+	-	+	+
6. Flowers	-	-	+	+
7. Dominant sporophyte	+	-	+	+
8. True roots	+	-	+	+

Step 1 Reorganise the rows so that there is a decreasing number of + symbols in each row. Don't worry if you don't know what a photosynthetic gametophyte is – it is the + and – symbols that matter, not the actual characteristics.

Characteristic	Organism			
	fern	moss	daisy	tulip
3. Chlorophyll	+	+	+	+
5. Vascular tissue	+	-	+	+
7. Dominant sporophyte	+	-	+	+
8. True roots	+	-	+	+
6. Flowers	-	-	+	+
1. Photosynthetic gametophyte	+	+	-	-
2. Dispersal by seeds	-	-	+	+
4. Dispersal by spores	+		-	-

Step 2 We now see that characteristics 5, 7 and 8 go + - + +. We need to move the + symbols to the right so we swap the fern and moss columns.

Characteristic	Organism			
	moss	fern	daisy	tulip
3. Chlorophyll	+	+	+	+
5. Vascular tissue	-	+	+	+
7. Dominant sporophyte	-	+	+	+
8. True roots	-	+	+	+
6. Flowers	-	-	+	+
1. Photosynthetic gametophyte	+	+	-	-
2. Dispersal by seeds	-	-	+	+
4. Dispersal by spores	+	+	-	-

Step 3 We can now build the cladogram. Characteristic 3 is the base one because all four organisms possess it. The next row shared by all is characteristic 5 along with characteristics 7 and 8. The last branch point comes with characteristics 2 and 6.

Characteristic	Organism			
	moss	**fern**	**daisy**	**tulip**
3. Chlorophyll	+	+	+	+
1. Photosynthetic gametophyte	+	+	-	-
4. Dispersal by spores	+	+	-	-
5. Vascular tissue	-	+	+	+
7. Dominant sporophyte	-	+	+	+
8. True roots	-	+	+	+
6. Flowers	-	-	+	+
2. Dispersal by seeds	-	-	+	+

Note that 1 and 4 are not used. This is because they are characteristics that are lost.

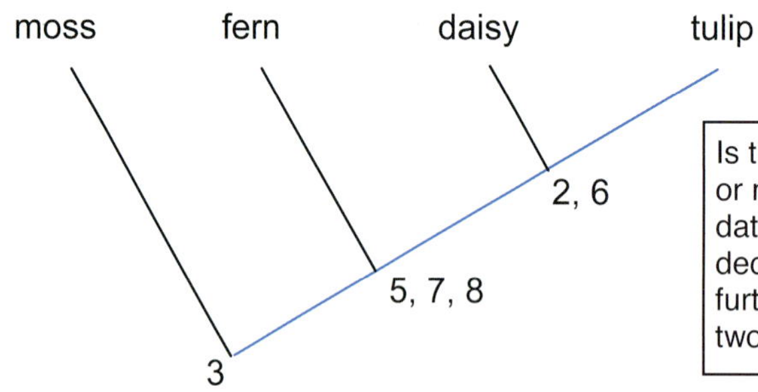

Is the order moss, fern, daisy, tulip, or moss, fern, tulip, daisy? The data we have does not allow us to decide. We would need some further characteristics from these two plants.

Note that I have used a different way of drawing the cladogram. This is much easier and quicker than the other form, but this is shown below for comparison. You can use either in an exam. Also note that the blue diagonal line up to the right must end in an organism, in this case, tulip.

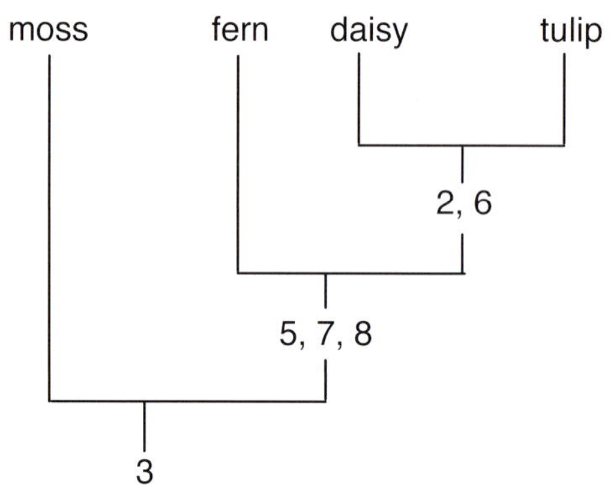

Problem 2

Characteristic	Organism						
	lizard	Orangutan	lamprey	bear	sunfish	Amphioxus	newt
1. jaws	+	+	-	+	+	-	+
2. mammary glands	-	+	-	+	-	-	-
3. opposable thumbs	-	+	-	-	-	-	-
4. amniotic egg	+	+	-	+	-	-	-
5. backbone	+	+	+	+	+	-	+
6. four limbs	+	+	-	+	-	-	+

Characteristic	Organism						
	Amphioxus	lamprey	sunfish	newt	lizard	bear	Orangutan
5. backbone	-	+	+	+	+	+	+
1. jaws	-	-	+	+	+	+	+
6. four limbs	-	-	-	+	+	+	+
4. amniotic egg	-	-	-	-	+	+	+
2. mammary glands	-	-	-	-	-	+	+
3. opposable thumbs	-	-	-	-	-	-	+

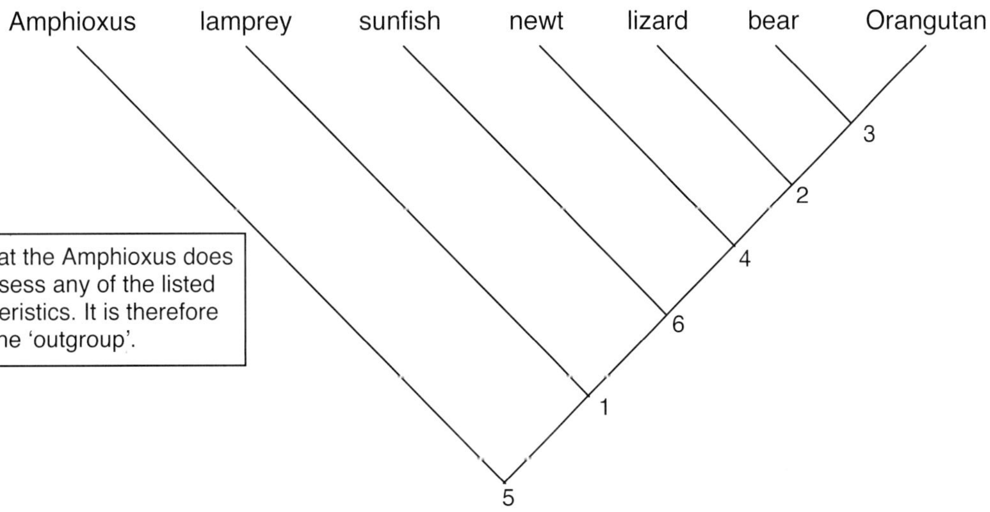

Note that the Amphioxus does not possess any of the listed characteristics. It is therefore called the 'outgroup'.

Problem 3

Characteristic	Organism						
	salamander	chimpanzee	perch	mouse	lizard	pigeon	hagfish
1. Feathers	-	-	-	-	-	+	-
2. Fur	-	+	-	+	-	-	-
3. Mammary glands	-	+	-	+	-	-	-
4. Lungs	+	+	-	+	+	+	-
5. Claws or nails	-	+	-	+	+	+	-
6. Jaws	+	+	+	+	+	+	-

Characteristic	Organism						
	hagfish	perch	salamander	lizard	pigeon	mouse	chimpanzee
6. Jaws	-	+	+	+	+	+	+
4. Lungs	-	-	+	+	+	+	+
5. Claws or nails	-	-	-	+	+	+	+
2. Fur	-	-	-	-	-	+	+
3. Mammary glands	-	-	-	-	-	+	+
1. Feathers	-	-	-	-	+	-	-

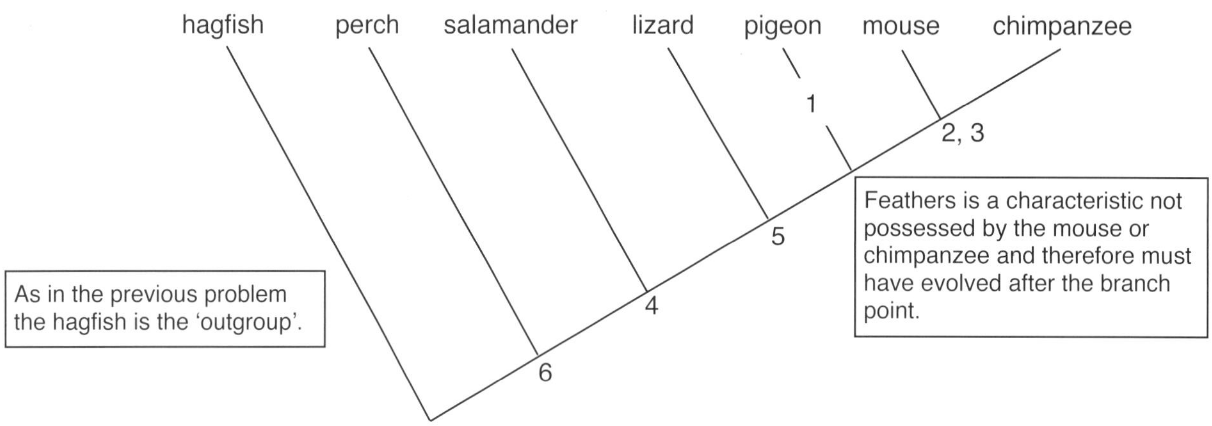

Problem 4

Characteristic	Organism						
	sharks	ray-finned fish	primates	rodents	crocodiles	birds	amphibians
1. 2 post-orbital fenestrae	-	-	-	-	+	+	-
2. vertebrae	+	+	+	+	+	+	+
3. four limbs	-	-	+	+	+	+	+
4. amniotic egg	-	-	+	+	+	+	-
5. hair	-	-	+	+	-	-	-
6. bony skeleton	-	+	+	+	+	+	+

Characteristic	Organism						
	sharks	ray-finned fish	amphibians	crocodiles	birds	rodents	primates
2. vertebrae	+	+	+	+	+	+	+
6. bony skeleton	-	+	+	+	+	+	+
3. four limbs	-	-	+	+	+	+	+
4. amniotic egg	-	-	-	+	+	+	+
1. two post-orbital fenestrae	-	-	-	+	+	-	-
5. hair	-	-	-	-	-	+	+

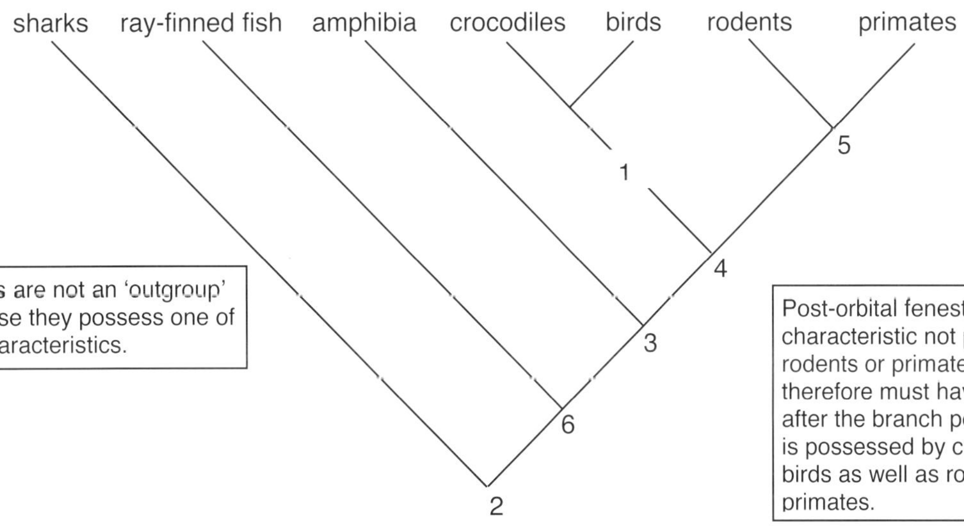

Sharks are not an 'outgroup' because they possess one of the characteristics.

Post-orbital fenestrae is a characteristic not possessed by rodents or primates. This therefore must have evolved after the branch point 4, which is possessed by crocodiles and birds as well as rodents and primates.